COPYRIGHT

Printed in the United States of America
EOJ Publishing, Annapolis, Maryland
First Printing, 2020
Illustrator: Fred Cabreira
Book Cover Design and Formatting : SankalpArt
(www.sankalpart.com)
Watercolor Illustration Technique
Editor: Gary Rubin
ISBN : 978-1-7352495-3-7
Little Doo-Doo: A Better Tomorrow
BookGasm Store
Email: BlogDaRAJ@gmail.com
Website: www.littledoodoo.com
San Diego County, CA

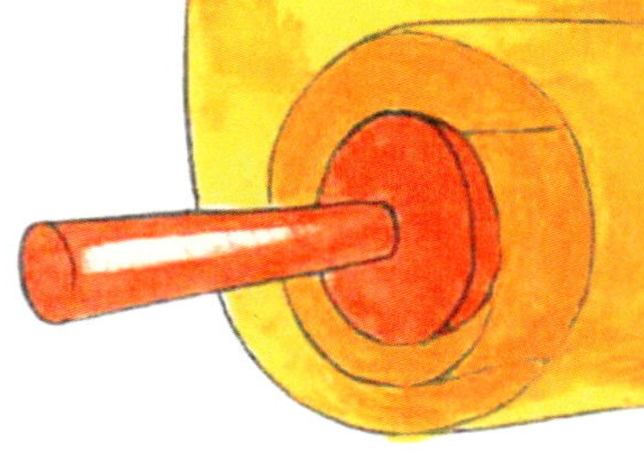

Dear
Parents & Readers,
Greetings!

A CITY WITHOUT WALLS is the third book, in a series about Talking to kids about difficult subjects.

UNIQUE – NOT WEIRD! - is the first book. It talks about –race and ethnicity.

NAVAL WARSHIP HIDDEN TREASURE -is the second book. It talks about the contributions and sacrifices made by military children and their families.

The stories in this collection represent real conversations within the context of our family.

Children have questions! When your child asks about a person they see sleeping on the street, or someone resting on the sidewalk with their belongings, it can be difficult to answer but from a child's perspective, it's simple curiosity.

As parents, the ideal answer should include concepts such as empathy, compassion and social responsibility. If you want to explain a complex issue like homelessness in a way your child will understand, it's best to be well prepared when the inevitable questions arise. Hopefully, this book will initiate ways to navigate a difficult conversation.

I suggest talking to your kid about homelessness before they encounter it for the first time. That way, they'll have a working understanding when they do meet a homeless person.This approach also gives parents more control over what exactly your kids learn about homelessness since they're learning it right from you, not friends or TV.

There are a few things you may want to avoid when talking about homelessness. It's a tricky subject, and only natural for kids to feel unsettled or upset by it. Though uncomfortable at times, avoid lying to your child about homelessness. Do not avoid their questions, try to keep your answers simple and age-appropriate, and do your best to answer honestly. After every talk, encourage your child if they have more questions about what you've talked about. Ask them to sum up what they've learned and this will help make sure your message was received the way you intended.

Homelessness is an important issue in our community,country and world. After learning about homelessness, most children become more compassionate, caring, and empathetic. It is important to dismantle stereotypes and reduce judgmental attitudes. Hopefully, your child will develop an appreciation for diversity, while recognizing widespread commonalities, as well as enhancing their capacity for critical thinking and moral reasoning. Engage your child in community initiatives and organizations. And, when the time comes, please vote for Little Doo-Doo. I can assure you she will be an honorable and committed first female President.

Much Love!

Regina

DEDICATION

I dedicate this book to my daughter Orlanda and honor the dreams of all other children.
Everybody has a dream, a goal or an aspiration that they wish would come true and I'm no different -- I
wanted to be a mom. Like a miracle, my little girl arrived and Orlanda (my Little Doo-Doo) is a dream
come true. Motherhood uncovered a passion lying dormant for over a decade.

As a mother who received a gift from heaven, I write these words to remind my baby girl the following:
Don't let anyone stop you from living your dreams or let fear prevent you from achieving your desires.
Remember, you are SMART, Black and beautiful and there's no contradiction in being ALL that! Believe
in yourself, follow your heart, and live your dreams.

Perhaps the most difficult part of parenthood is the realization I now have to live and lead.
I embrace the great privilege life allows and hope to leave a godly legacy that will last for generations!
Now more than ever, I made the choice to live my best life, to strive to achieve my best self because that
is the example for you and every child on earth.

How I live my life is the best way to teach you, and other children, how to live their lives.
Because of you, I made the decision to live my dream. I urge you to chase your dreams, as well.
My vote will always be yours!

With much
love!

Momma

Hello children,
I am Little **Doo-Doo** and I want to start this story by introducing you
to my family!

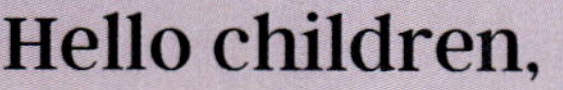

Ladies and gentlemen it is with great honor I introduce to you my amazing **daddy:** Big Don-Don.

I think my mom was lucky to have my dad marry her because he is so brown and so handsome!

If you are wondering why I love my daddy so much, here's why:

He is super-protective.
He teaches me how to be strong.
He says I am his princess and incessantly cares for me.
He told me I will always remain his little girl.

This is my lovely mother: **Momma Din-Din**

I think my daddy was lucky to have my momma marry him because she wants to make the world a better place and I was fortunate they found each other.

If you are wondering why I love my momma so much, here's why:
She does everything selflessly and perfectly.

She allows me to be me. I am my own person, not someone Momma wishes she would be. That means she loves me unconditionally, no matter what I do.

She knows everything, from how to make an omelet to the intricacies of cold fusion. My mother and I spend a Saturday morning trying to cook grandma's gumbo recipe. Momma said I am going to be tall as Grandma Linda is!

And, this is me!

Orlanda Johnson. Most known as **Little Doo-Doo**.

I love reading and writing.

I also have a Youtube Channel. I have no subscribers, yet I still have high self-esteem.

When I grow up, I will be a doctor but I don't know which type of doctor. However, my real calling is to lead.

Yes, I will be the boss! I already know how to boss people around! I learned it with daddy!

Little Doo-Doo was so happy when momma told her: "It is a beautiful San Diego day!"

2

Once there, Little Doo-Doo noticed a homeless person, poorly dressed and said out loud, "Momma, that lady is so scary.," after hearing her loud voice.

Momma, trying to explain simply and honestly, said to her 5-year old: "I think she is having a hard time. Sometimes people need to yell or scream. I think that's what she's doing."

"Why, when I yell and scream you tell me it is not nice?" Little Doo-Doo asked. "I am your mother and I need to tell you what the right thing to do is."

3

Holding Little Doo-Doo in her arms, momma tried to calm her down: "Momma is here. You have nothing to fear!

Holding Little Doo-Doo they arrived in The Aviation & Space Museum

where they enjoyed seeing the amazing
exhibits that afternoon.

On the way back home, Little Doo-Doo noticed a family with children resting on the sidewalk with their belongings. Pointing to the family Little Doo-Doo asked: ``Momma, who are these people?''

Momma looked into Little Doo-Doo's eyes and said: "They are homeless who need help. Don't point to people and call them `these people.' "

"Why momma?"
Little Doo-Doo
asked.

Momma answered: "Many times we don't know enough about others, especially when they live differently from us. When we say `these people' it means that we don't know enough and ... "

Before momma finished, Little Doo-Doo ran to the homeless family

and asked: "Hello! Who are you?
My mother said I don't know you
enough. I want to get to know
you. Can we play?"

Momma was caught by surprise and didn't know what to say but tried:

The homeless lady smiled and then looked at Little Doo-Doo: "What do you want to know?"

Little Doo-Doo, enjoying her attention, said: "Is that true you live here?"

Momma interrupted: "You should ask for their names before any other questions."

"What's your name?" Little Doo-Doo asked.

12

The family introduced themselves: "Hi, my name is Jessica. This is my husband, Bernardo.
This is Olivia, she's 5 and Mia is 4.
We are from Mexico. We live on the streets and we are blessed to be here.
Someday, we hope to have a house!"

"Momma, can we move to the streets and be their neighbors?" Little Doo-Doo asked.

Jessica laughed at Little Doo-Doo and said: "No. We should move into a house and be your neighbors!"

Little Doo-Doo asked: "In Mexico,
did you have a home?"

Jessica replied: "We had a place to live but we couldn't stay there.
There are reasons someone becomes homeless.
"There may be abuse, violence, unjust policies, family troubles, poverty, illness or drugs".
16

Little Doo-Doo proudly said: "My mother is from Brazil but she hasa home and a job!"

Little Doo-Doo asked: "Why don't you find a job and a home for your family?"

Jessica replied: "Nice!"

Little Doo-Doo, that is hard to answer." Momma said.

17

Jessica smiled and said: We hope and pray to find jobs and a home for our family. We are waiting upon the Lord.

18

Little Doo-Doo, out loud said: "God, hurry up! Can't you see they don't have a place to live? Why are you taking so long?"

19

That response made Jessica and her husband laugh.

Momma tried to explain: "Sometimes, things are not simple to fix."

20

"But, momma you said God can do anything." Little Doo-Doo reminded her momma.

"Why is God not doing anything?"

Momma tried to explain: "Sometimes God seems not to do anything because he is giving us an opportunity to do something."

"Ok, momma I am going to give Olivia and Mia my toys. I also want to bake pies and cookies for them. And, as soon as I become the first female President of the United States, I will give them a palace". Jessica and Bernardo had tears in their eyes and visibly enjoyed Little Doo-Doo's future plans.

As momma and Little Doo-Doo were leaving, Bernardo said: "Little Doo-Doo, count on us. My family will vote for you!"

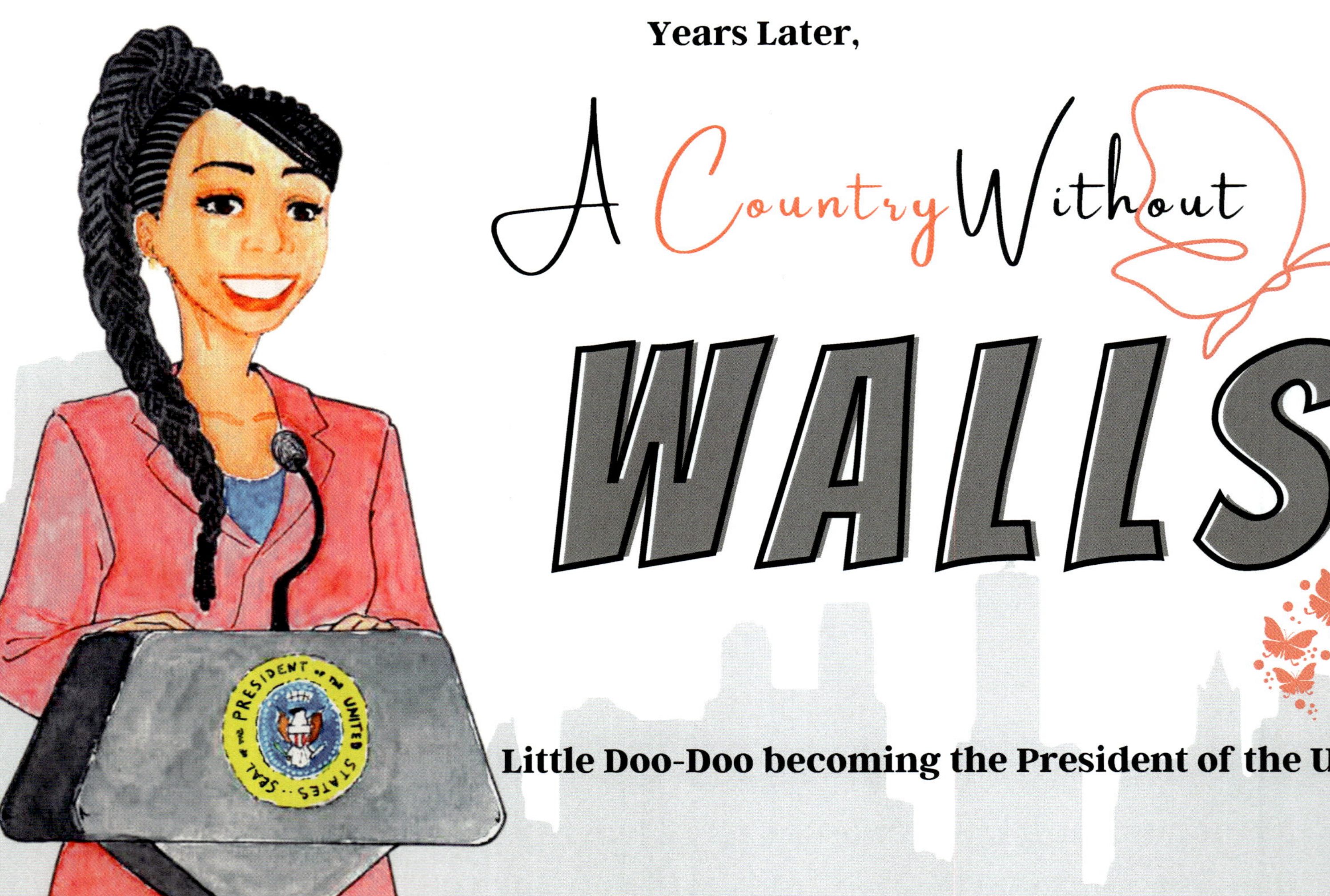
Years Later,

A Country Without

WALLS

Little Doo-Doo becoming the President of the USA!

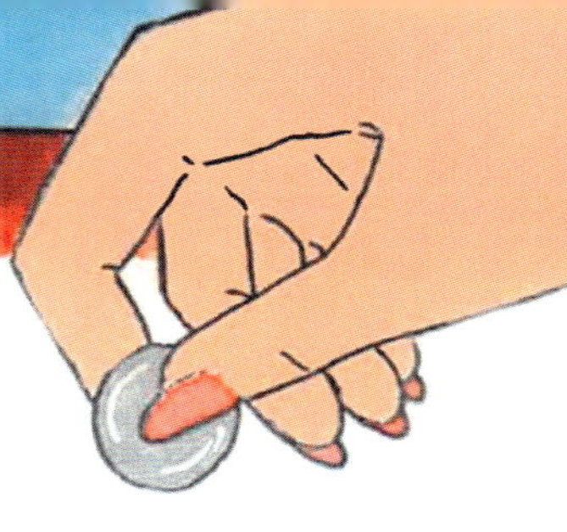

Thank You!

Thanks be to God for making this project possible!

Eric Johnson - *Husband & Best* Friend for your support and love.

Gary Rubin - *Editor* for your dedication and empowerment.

Fred Cabreira - *Illustrator* for your creativity and humility.

Prof. Sankalp Shrivastava - *Design & Format* for your magic and beauty!

Dr. Regina A. Johnson

AUTHOR'S CONTACT INFORMATION

As a reader of this book, you are the most important critic and commentator. We value your opinion and want to know what we did right, what we could do better, what different topics you'd like to see published, and any other words of wisdom you're willing to share.

As the author, I welcome your comments. You can send an email to let me know what you liked or didn't like about this children's book and series.   Let us know how we can improve. When you write, please be sure to include this book's title, ISBN, and your contact information. I will carefully review your comments and share them with the editor and illustrator who are part of the team who worked on the book.
Due to the high volume of emails, I may not reply to every message.

Author: Regina Johnson

Email: BlogdaRAJ@gmail.com

Made in the USA
Coppell, TX
27 September 2020

38784192R00024